CONTENTS

What is a mummy?	4
Air dryer	6
Making a mummy	8
Ice men	10
Bog bodies	12
Smokin' mummies	14
Good as new?	16
Mummy misery	18
Under wraps	20
Back from the dead	22
Celebrity mummies	24
Fakes and mistakes	26
Modern mummies	28
Glossary	30
Further information	31
Index	32

What is a mummy?

Mummies stumble around, wrapped in bandages, preying on human flesh – at least they do in the movies. Real life is different, but it can be just as gruesome.

Your body is designed to rot, or decompose. When you die, the **bacteria** that have been living quietly inside your body really go to town. They start to eat you – from the inside out!

The rotting process has to be stopped for a body to become a mummy. If a body is mummified it can last for thousands of years.

A healthy body is full of bacteria – they won't start to eat you until you're dead.

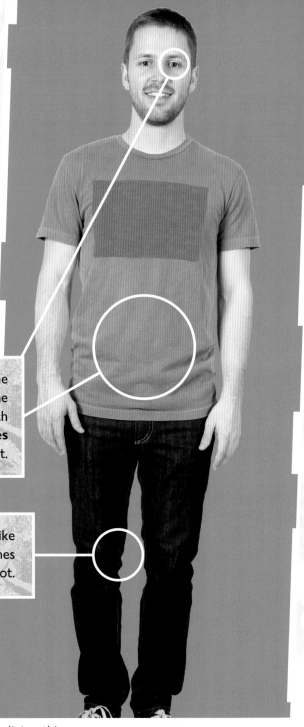

Soft parts of the body such as the eyes, stomach and **intestines** rot away first.

Hard parts like teeth and bones are last to rot.

bacteria tiny cells that can both help and harm living things

EXTREME

Mummies

Mysteries of the Ancient World

Paul Harrison

Produced for A & C Black by

Monkey Puzzle Media Ltd
48 York Avenue
Hove BN3 1JD, UK

Published by A & C Black Publishers Limited
36 Soho Square, London W1D 3QY

Paperback published 2010
First published 2009
Copyright © 2009 A & C Black Publishers Limited

ISBN 978-1-4081-1260-1 (hardback)
ISBN 978-1-4081-1988-4 (paperback)

Editor: Susie Brooks
Design: Mayer Media Ltd
Picture research: Lynda Lines
Series consultants: Jane Turner and James de Winter

This book is produced using paper that is made
from wood grown in managed, sustainable forests.
It is natural, renewable and recyclable. The logging
and manufacturing processes conform to the
environmental regulations of the country of origin.

Printed in Malaysia by Tien Wah Press (Pte.) Ltd

Picture acknowledgements
Alamy pp. 18 (North Wind Picture Archives), 26–27
(Dennis Cox); Art Archive p. 26 left (Musée du
Louvre, Paris/Gianni Dagli Orti); Camera Press pp.
15 (Gamma/Duclos Alexis), 17 (New China News
Agency); Corbis pp. 6 bottom left (Claudio
Castellon/epa), 11 (Vienna Report Agency), 14
(Chris Rainier), 28 (Ryan Pyle/None); Adam Husted
p. 21; iStockphoto p. 4; MPM Images pp. 5 bottom
right (Universal Pictures), 12, 16 (Smithsonian
National Museum of Natural History), 24 left
(University College London); National Geographic
Society pp. 8 left, 8 right; Rex Features pp. 1 (Sipa
Press), 10 (Sipa Press), 19 (Sipa Press), 24–25 (Sipa
Press), 29 (Wotjek Laski); Science Photo Library pp.
9 (Christian Jegou/Publiphoto Diffusion), 13 (Silkeborg
Museum, Denmark/Munoz-Yague), 20 (Alexander
Tsiaras), 23 (British Museum/Munoz-Yague);
Topfoto.co.uk p. 22; Werner Forman Archive p. 5
left (E Strouhal/Naprstek Muaseum, Prague);
Wikimedia Commons pp. 6–7 (British Museum).

The front cover shows a mummy in the catacombs
of Palermo, Italy (MPM Images).

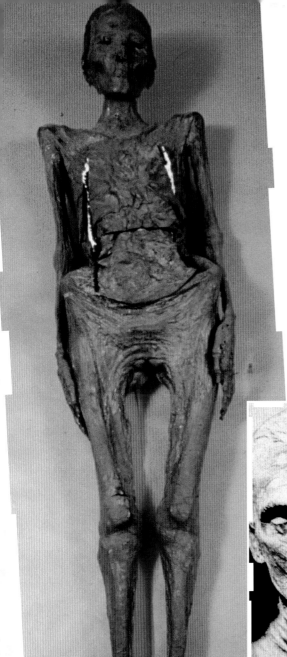

Movie mummies!

In 1932, the horror movie *The Mummy* came out. Boris Karloff played an ancient Egyptian priest who had been brought back to life. Even Boris's *own* mummy wouldn't have recognized him – he was wrapped in bandages! Mummies have been a hit at the movies ever since.

She may not look that healthy, but this mummy is over 1,000 years old.

A poster for the first major mummy movie.

intestines the tube from your stomach to your bottom

Air dryer

Mummies are sometimes made by accident. If the air is dry enough, bodies dry out instead of rotting – and become mummies.

Watery wonder

Between 55 and 65 per cent of an adult human's body is made of water.

This air-dried mummy from China is curled up, just as he died.

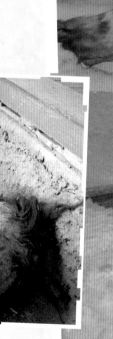

withered dried out **preserve** to keep, or make last

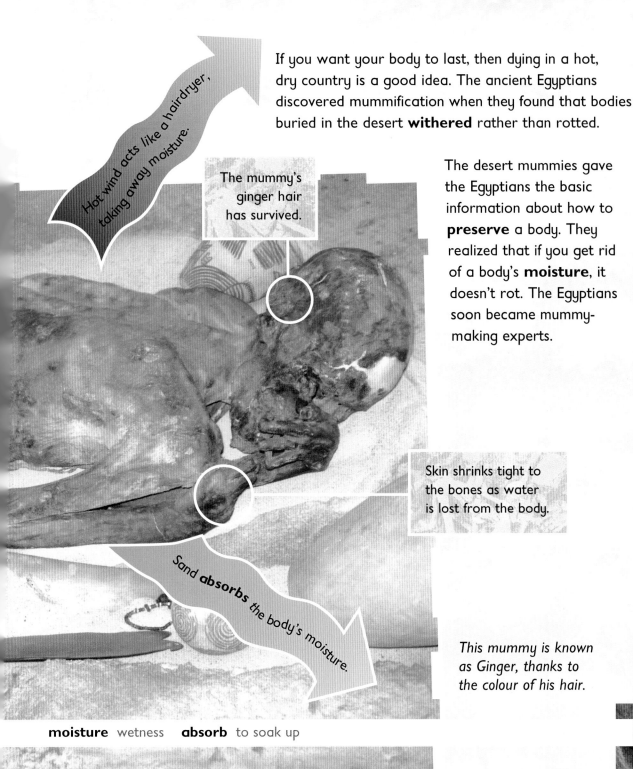

If you want your body to last, then dying in a hot, dry country is a good idea. The ancient Egyptians discovered mummification when they found that bodies buried in the desert **withered** rather than rotted.

The desert mummies gave the Egyptians the basic information about how to **preserve** a body. They realized that if you get rid of a body's **moisture**, it doesn't rot. The Egyptians soon became mummy-making experts.

Hot wind acts like a hairdryer, taking away moisture.

The mummy's ginger hair has survived.

Skin shrinks tight to the bones as water is lost from the body.

Sand **absorbs** the body's moisture.

This mummy is known as Ginger, thanks to the colour of his hair.

moisture wetness **absorb** to soak up

Making a mummy

What do salt and a long metal hook have in common? Well, they are two of the things that the ancient Egyptians used to make bodies last for thousands of years.

Mummification stage 1: **Organs** *such as the brain, lungs and liver contain lots of water so are removed.*

Large hook pulls the brain out through the nose.

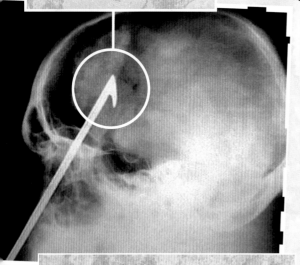

Poor show

Mummification was very expensive, so poor Egyptians had to make do with being buried in the sand.

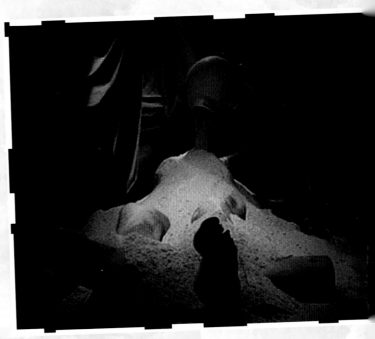

Stage 2: The body is dried out for 40 days in a salt called natron.

organs parts of the body that do special jobs

Mask will cover the mummy's face.

Organs are stored in jars.

Not so tight!

Body is stuffed with cloth to keep its shape.

The Egyptians believed that when people died, they went on to an **afterlife**. This made it important for bodies to be preserved. Mummification became a religious ceremony, carried out by priests saying prayers and casting spells.

If the whole point was to make bodies last, then the Egyptians did a great job. They had really worked out the best way of drying a body so that it wouldn't rot.

Stage 3: The body is wrapped in bandages and prepared for burial.

afterlife life after death

Ice men

The weather high up in the mountains is icy cold. It can have the same effect as a giant freezer when it comes to dead bodies – keeping them fresh for ages.

In the past, people from Peru used the cold mountain air to mummify their dead relatives.

When two hikers found the **corpse** of a man in the Alps, they thought it was a recent body. It turned out to be a 5,300-year-old mummy! How and why he died remained a mystery for years. Eventually scientists discovered the end of a **flint** arrow buried in his shoulder, proving that the ice man had been murdered a long time ago.

corpse a dead body   **flint** a type of stone used for old tools and weapons

"Otzi" the ice mummy is more than 5,000 years old.

Bodies in the freezer

Some people pay to be frozen when they die, hoping they might be brought back to life in the future! This is called cyronics.

Cold mountain air freezes the body.

Otzi's last meal of meat and bread is still inside his stomach.

Tree **pollen** on the body shows that Otzi died during the spring.

Bacteria don't like the cold, so Otzi's body did not rot.

pollen a powdery substance that plants use to reproduce

11

Bog bodies

Getting trapped in a bog would be bad news – you could get sucked down and drown. On the plus side, your body might become a famous mummy!

*This bog body has been flattened by the heavy **peat**.*

Bog water dyes hair ginger.

Grisly secrets

Some bodies found in bogs seem to show that they had been killed as a punishment, or even **sacrificed**.

You'd think that a body in a really wet place like a bog would rot quickly – but that's not what happens at all. Instead bodies in bogs get pickled, like pickled onions, before they rot.

There's very little air in bog water, and the bacteria that rot bodies need air to survive. Also, the water is full of plants that make the water slightly **acid** – like the vinegar that onions are pickled in.

peat mixture of rotting plants and water   **sacrificed** killed as part of a religious ceremony

"Tollund Man" lived 6,000 years ago – until he was hanged and buried in a bog.

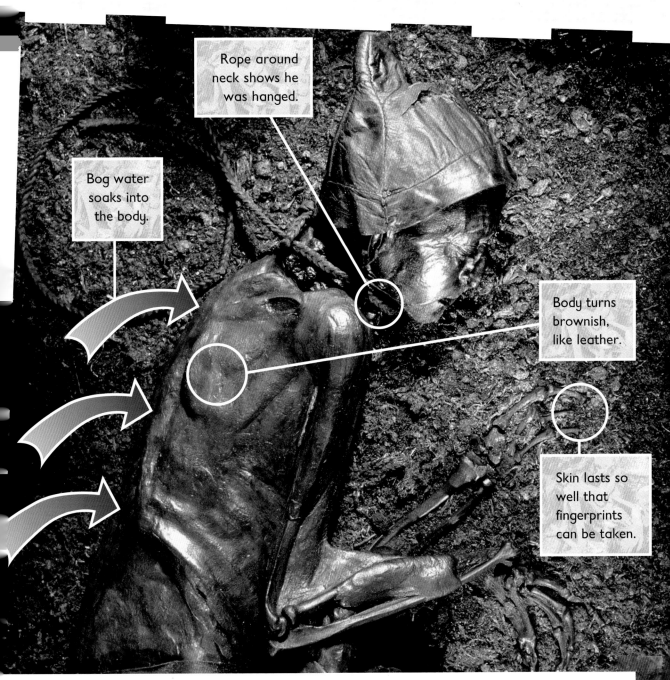

Rope around neck shows he was hanged.

Bog water soaks into the body.

Body turns brownish, like leather.

Skin lasts so well that fingerprints can be taken.

acid substance that can cause chemical changes

Smokin' mummies

Death doesn't always mean saying goodbye forever. Some people mummify relatives so they can still visit them – even though they're no longer alive!

Smoked mummies from Papua New Guinea do a lot of sitting around.

In Papua New Guinea, dead bodies are preserved using smoke – a bit like a butcher smokes ham. The mummies are then displayed in a high place that overlooks the village, or placed in local huts. In this way, the villagers feel that the dead are still part of their **community**.

Bad – and good

Tobacco smoke is bad for your health – but great for preserving dead bodies!

community a group of people who live near each other   **dehydrate** to dry out

Good as new?

Fangtastic tales

Vampire legends might have their roots in the discovery of well-preserved **adipocere** corpses.

Imagine opening an old coffin and finding a well-preserved body inside! It sounds like a scene from a vampire movie, but it can really happen.

A coffin and where it is buried can have surprising effects on a corpse – especially if an **airtight** coffin is buried in damp, cold ground. In these conditions, the fats inside the body can turn into a waxy or soap-like substance called adipocere. This can make the body look as if it has stopped rotting altogether.

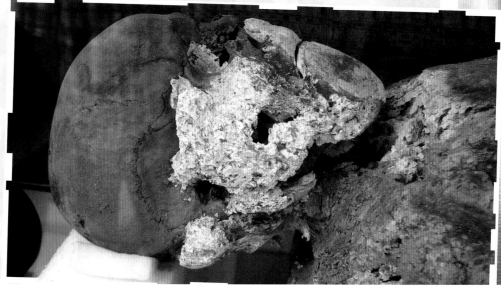

The "Soap Man" is a body preserved by adipocere.

adipocere name given to body fats when they turn soapy or waxy after death

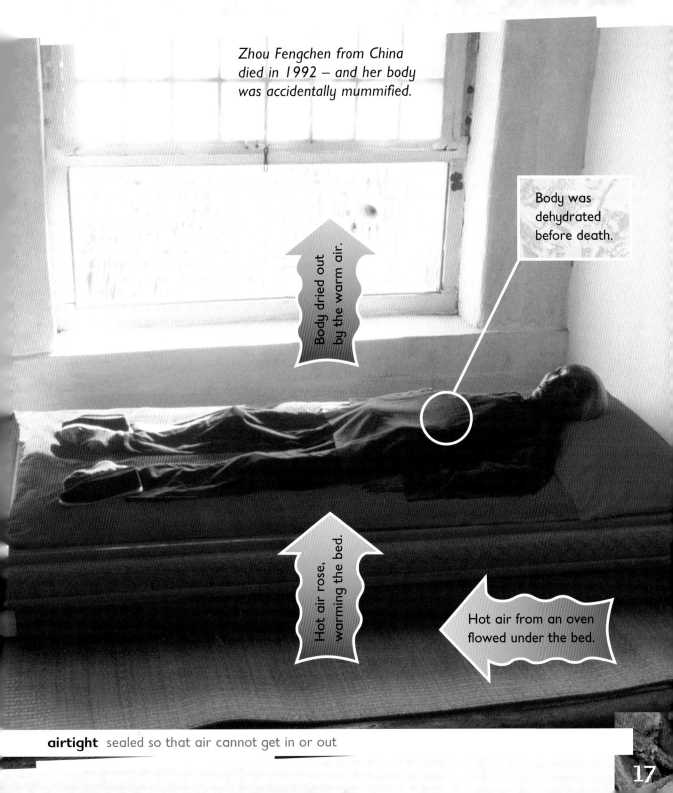

Zhou Fengchen from China died in 1992 – and her body was accidentally mummified.

Body was dehydrated before death.

Body dried out by the warm air.

Hot air rose, warming the bed.

Hot air from an oven flowed under the bed.

airtight sealed so that air cannot get in or out

Mummy misery

How would you like to be stuck in a glass case – in the nude – for people to stare at? That's what some mummies have to put up with!

No fuel like an old fuel

As mummies are very dry, it is claimed that some were burnt as fuel for steam trains!

Throughout history, mummies have been treated terribly by people who didn't realize (or didn't care) what they were handling:

- Mummies have been sold by **tomb** robbers to wealthy collectors.
- Some have been ground up and used in medicine.
- In Guanajuato, Mexico, people had to pay to stay buried! If relatives could not afford the fees then the bodies were dug up and put on display in a museum.

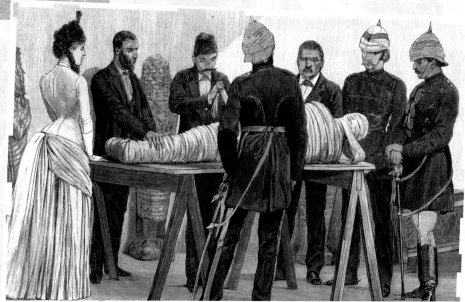

Parties to watch a mummy being unwrapped were popular in Victorian Britain.

tomb a burial chamber

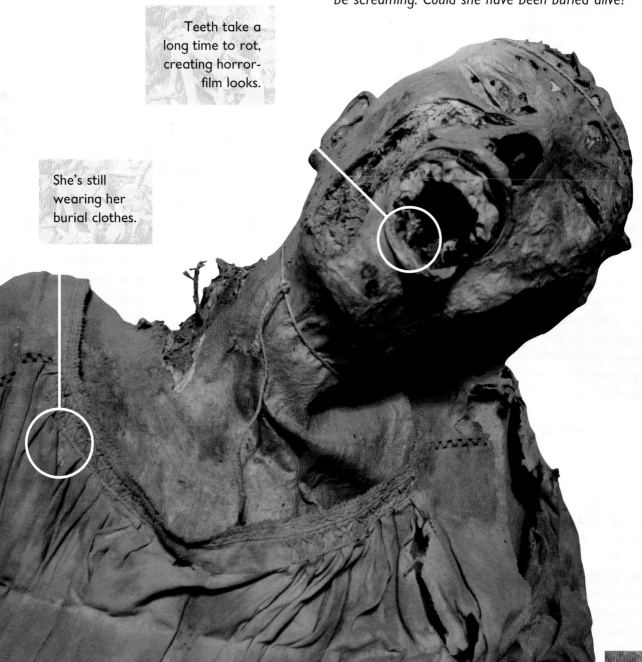

This Mexican mummy from Guanajuato appears to be screaming. Could she have been buried alive?

Teeth take a long time to rot, creating horror-film looks.

She's still wearing her burial clothes.

Under wraps

Taking a mummy to hospital seems a bit odd — after all, it's a bit late for a doctor to do anything. It's not too late for archaeologists, though.

Archaeologists use hi-tech hospital machinery to look inside mummies — without having to remove any bandages. **X-ray machines** and **CT scanners** beam rays of energy, called X-rays, through the mummy. Hard bits, such as bones, absorb the rays, while soft bits, such as skin, let the rays through. The results are then shown on a photograph.

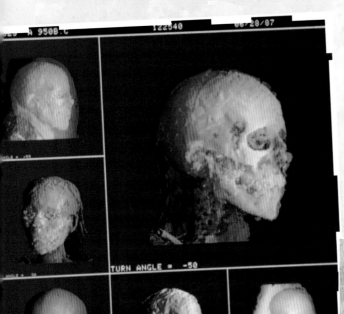

CT scans show the skull of an Egyptian mummy called Ta-bes.

Mystery solved

Many people thought that the ancient Egyptian King Tutankhamun was murdered. In fact, modern investigations found he had died from an infected leg wound.

archaeologist someone who studies ancient peoples by looking at their remains

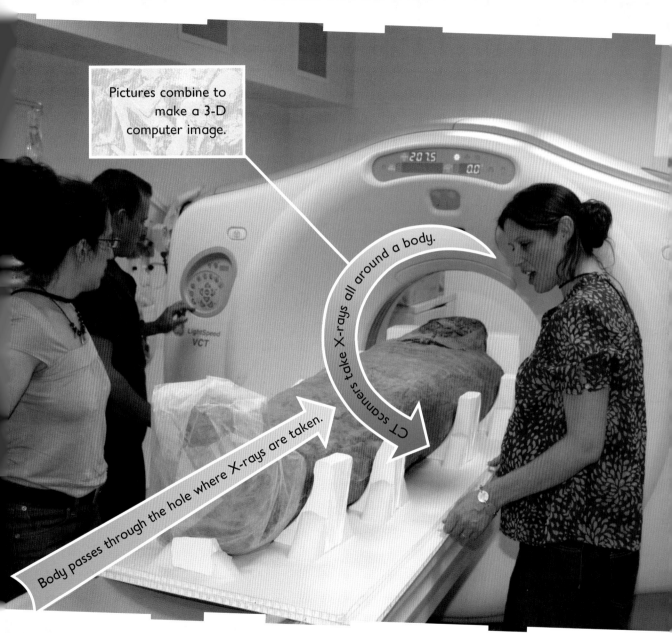

Mummies don't even have to leave their coffins to be scanned.

Pictures combine to make a 3-D computer image.

CT scanners take X-rays all around a body.

Body passes through the hole where X-rays are taken.

X-ray machines and **CT scanners** machines that take pictures of the inside of a body

Back from the dead

Do looks matter? Archaeologists think so, which is why they spend so much time studying mummies to work out what they might have looked like.

Reconstructions have been made from this 2,000 year-old bog body, known as Lindow Man.

1 Skull is usually copied first.

reconstruction a copy of something that no longer survives

2 Flesh and muscles are added next, using local people as a guide to facial features.

Reconstructing the faces of people who have died is a skill that the police often use when solving crimes. It's useful for archaeologists too. They can get a good idea of what a mummy might have looked like when it was alive. Sometimes looks can tell them other things about a person, too.

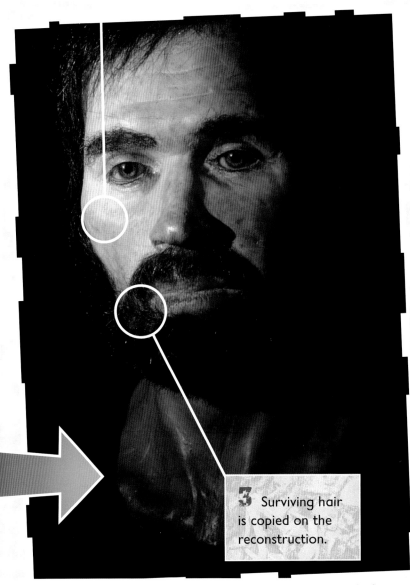

3 Surviving hair is copied on the reconstruction.

Hand history

Archaeologists look at different parts of mummies for clues about their lives. Rough hands or fingernails show that the person probably did manual work.

This is what Lindow Man might have looked like in life.

manual work working with your hands, for example farming

Celebrity mummies

Important people – including kings, priests, and even politicians – have been mummified throughout history.

Russian leader Vladimir Lenin's body is on display in Moscow.

Face and hands occasionally show signs of rotting.

My feet smell!

Jeremy Bentham's real head used to sit between the feet of his mummy.

No one really knows why the **philosopher** Jeremy Bentham wanted to be mummified. But we do know that his head fell off in the process, and had to be replaced with a wax one!

The Russian political leader Lenin had no idea that he would be mummified. On his death, the government decided to preserve his body so the Russian people could pay their respects.

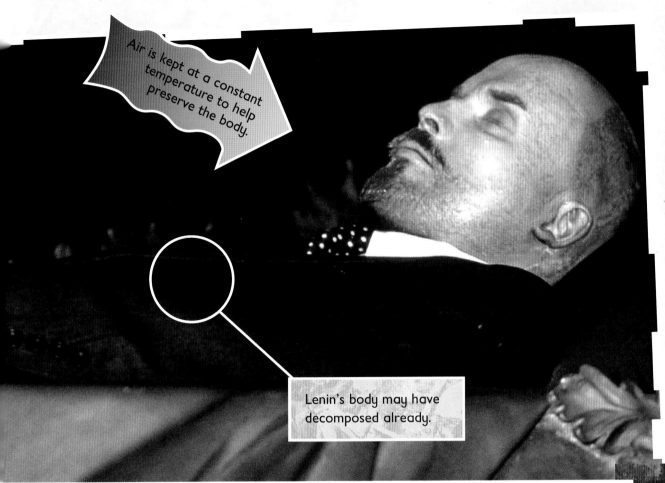

Air is kept at a constant temperature to help preserve the body.

Lenin's body may have decomposed already.

philosopher someone who thinks about and studies life

Fakes and mistakes

When is a mummy not a mummy? When it's a fake or a mistake! Sometimes mummies are not what they appear...

Occasionally museums have discovered that the mummies they have on display are actually fakes — nothing more than bandages stuffed with cloths. They had been conned!

Not all empty body coverings are fakes, though. In some cases, real attempts to mummify bodies have failed — leaving nothing but the clothes or coffin the body was buried in.

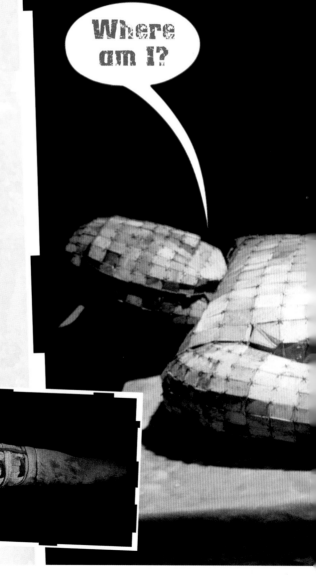

Where am I?

Faking a small animal mummy is easier than faking a human mummy.

jade a valuable gemstone

A Chinese emperor once lay inside this head-to-toe jade suit.

Animal antics

The Egyptians mummified animals they thought were **sacred**, such as cats, crocodiles and even bulls.

Suit is made from jade plates, sewn together with gold thread.

Jade was thought to preserve bodies — but unfortunately it doesn't.

sacred important or holy in a particular religion

Modern mummies

Believe it or not, people are still being mummified today – though things have moved on since ancient Egyptian times!

A plastinated body gets ready for an exhibition.

A German professor called Gunther von Hagens has discovered a new way of making mummies. He uses a process called plastination.

Plastination works by **dissolving** all of a body's fat, and replacing the body's water with liquid plastic. Once plastinated, the mummies go on display in museums and galleries around the world. Being dead has become a great way of attracting visitors!

Plastic pets

Any living thing can be plastinated, from tiny insects to large animals such as horses.

dissolve to break down a solid in a liquid

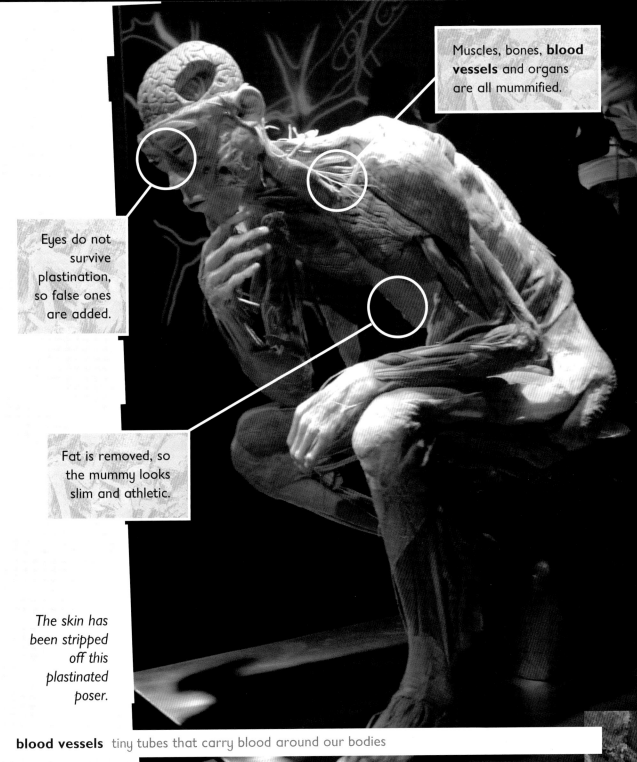

Muscles, bones, **blood vessels** and organs are all mummified.

Eyes do not survive plastination, so false ones are added.

Fat is removed, so the mummy looks slim and athletic.

The skin has been stripped off this plastinated poser.

blood vessels tiny tubes that carry blood around our bodies

Glossary

absorb to soak up

acid substance that can cause chemical changes

adipocere name given to body fats when they turn soapy or waxy after death

afterlife life after death

airtight sealed so that air cannot get in or out

archaeologist someone who studies ancient peoples by looking at their remains

bacteria tiny cells that can both help and harm living things

blood vessels tiny tubes that carry blood around our bodies

community a group of people who live near each other

corpse a dead body

CT scanners machines that take 3-D pictures of the inside of a body

dehydrate to dry out

dissolve to break down a solid in a liquid

flint a type of stone used for old tools and weapons

intestines the tube from your stomach to your bottom

jade a valuable gemstone

manual work working with your hands, for example farming

moisture wetness

organs parts of the body that do special jobs

peat mixture of rotting plants and water

philosopher someone who thinks about and studies life

pollen a powdery substance that plants use to reproduce

preserve to keep, or make last

reconstruction a copy of something that no longer survives

sacred important or holy in a particular religion

sacrificed killed as part of a religious ceremony

tomb a burial chamber

withered dried out

X-ray machines machines that take pictures of the inside of a body

Further information

Books

Mummy by James Putnam
(Dorling Kindersley, 2004)
A good overview of
different types of mummy.

***The Complete Book of
Mummies*** by Claire
Llewellyn (Wayland, 2001)
Looks at how mummies –
including animal mummies –
are made and studied.

Mummies and Pyramids
by Sam Taplin (Usbourne,
2001)
Lots on Egyptian mummies
as well as others – with
handy internet links.

***Bog Bodies: Mummies
and Curious Corpses*** by
Natalie Jane Prior (Allen
and Unwin, 1996)
Discover lots of different
mummies made in lots of
different ways.

***My Best Book of
Mummies*** by Philip Steele
(Kingfisher Books, 2000)
Good information on
Egyptian mummies covering
all the major areas.

Websites

www.mummytombs.com
This site describes different
kinds of mummies from all
over the world.

www.britishmuseum.org
Try the British Museum
site for Egyptian mummies
(humans and animals) and
the Lindow Man.

**www.carnegiemnh.org/
exhibits/egypt/index.htm**
The Carnegie Museum has
a lot on ancient Egypt.

**www.voxel-man.de/
gallery/virtual_mummy/**
See how a mummy can be
reconstructed using a CT
scanner. There is actual
footage of an Egyptian
mummy being scanned,
along with the results.

**http://video.
nationalgeographic.com
/video/player/specials/
in-the-field-specials/
ceruti-mummy.html**
Watch a video about
the discovery of
Peruvian mummies.

Films

**BEWARE! Some of
these films are scary!**

***The Curse of the
Mummy's Tomb***
directed by Michael
Carreras (Hammer, 1964)
An old-fashioned horror film
in which a mummy taken to
England comes back to life.

The Mummy directed
by Stephen Sommers
(Universal, 1999)
Treasure hunters
accidentally awaken a
3,600-year-old Egyptian
mummy, with fatal results.

***The Mummy: Tomb of
the Dragon Emperor***
directed by Rob Cohen
(Universal, 2008)
An action adventure. Not
really about a mummy
as such – more like the
re-awakening of a cursed
Chinese Emperor.

Index

adipocere 16
afterlife 9
animal mummies 26, 27, 28
archaeologists 20, 22, 23

bacteria 4, 11, 12
bandages 5, 9, 20, 26
Bentham, Jeremy 24, 25
bog bodies 12–13, 22
bones 4, 7, 20, 29

China 6, 17, 27
cryonics 11
CT scanners 20, 21

dried mummies 6, 7, 15, 17

Egyptians 5, 7, 8–9, 20,
    27, 28

fat 16, 28, 29

hair 7, 12, 23

ice mummy 10–11

jade 26, 27

Lenin, Vladimir 24, 25
Lindow Man 22, 23

Mexico 18, 19
mummification 8–9
museums 18, 26, 28

natron 8

organs 8, 9, 29
Otzi 10–11

Papua New Guinea 14
Peru 10
Philippines 15
plastination 28–29

reconstructions 22, 23
rotting 4, 24, 25

sacrifice 12
skin 7, 13, 15, 20, 29
smoke 14, 15
Soap Man 16

teeth 4, 19
Tollund Man 13
tomb robbers 18
Tutankhamun 20

vampire legends 16
von Hagens, Gunther 28

water 6, 7, 8, 12, 28

X-ray machines 20, 21